Eyes Like Fire, Sword in Mouth

Armando Perez

INTRODUCTION

This book was forged in the fire of real encounters with God - moments of surrender, spiritual warfare, and revival that branded my life forever. It is not a book of stories, but a call to awakening. It is written as a summons - an invitation to return to holy fire, surrendered obedience, and the fullness of God's purpose. These pages carry encouragement for the weary, conviction for the distracted, and ignition for those who know they were made for more. The power of God presented here is not a theory to admire, but a flame to be encountered, a consuming fire that purifies, refines, and reignites all it touches.

Each chapter is a collision between heaven and earth, where poetic narrative meets divine truth, calling the reader out of complacency and into the burning reality of a life with Jesus.

This is not a book for the passive heart. It is a charge to rise, to burn, and to walk in the power and purity of the living God. It is a trumpet call for those who refuse to settle for ordinary Christianity, for those who long to see a generation set ablaze with holy fire.

Jesus made a way for our salvation, and He is the embodiment of our sanctification. When we commit to follow Him, the journey becomes a divine unveiling - one that only the Holy Spirit can empower us to walk out.

The finished work of the Cross takes us from sinner to saint. It was the love of an omnipotent and omnipresent God, one who was willing to sacrifice His own Son for all humanity. He purchased our forgiveness. All our sins, mistakes, and failures were placed upon one Man. His name is Jesus. He fulfilled everything needed to please the Father.

As Romans declares: *"God sent His own Son in the likeness of sinful flesh to be a sin offering." (Romans 8:3)* And again: *"By one man's disobedience many were made sinners, so by one man's obedience many will be made righteous." (Romans 5:19)*

We have been co-crucified, co-buried, and co-resurrected with Jesus, to live as co-heirs, fully united with Him. What unfathomable love, that He would endure the cross for us while we were still lost and still welcomes us with tender mercy even after every failed attempt to fill the void apart from Him.

This is the Gospel of Jesus Christ.
He calls us to believe, to turn from our ways, and to carry this message of hope and fire to the ends of the earth.

As you read the pages ahead, and through the stories, may your heart be awakened to the depths of His love. Because no matter what you face, and no matter what you are walking through, there is a King with ***fire in His eyes and a sword in His mouth*** - the One who walked through the depths and is relentlessly pursuing you with a love that will never let go.

Armando Perez

You are not forgotten, for you have been chosen and destined by Father God. The Holy Spirit has set you apart to be God's holy ones, obedient followers of Jesus Christ who have been gloriously sprinkled with his blood. May God's delightful grace and peace cascade over you many times over! - 1 Peter 1:2 TPT

TABLE OF CONTENTS

Hearts on Fire

They walked with their heads bowed, eyes to the ground,
Hearts heavy with loss, no hope to be found.
The road stretched long through shadows and doubt.
The Savior was gone, and the light had gone out.

A stranger drew near with steps sure and slow,
And truth began softly to shimmer and glow.
His words, like embers, awakened desire,
"Did not our hearts burn with heavenly fire?"

They saw not His face, yet His words rang true,
The nearness they once felt began breaking through.
And when He broke bread, their sorrow took flight.
The veil was torn by His radiant light.

Their eyes were opened, the truth made clear,
The One they had lost was suddenly here.
Conviction fell like the cleansing of rain,
They turned from dark sorrow and released all the shame.
What once had grown dim now grew even brighter,
They carried the message, with hearts on fire.

Did Not Our Hearts Burn Within Us?

In Luke 24, two disciples trudged the road to Emmaus, confused and grieving. They had heard the teachings, walked with the Savior, and witnessed the miraculous for three years. If we were to put it in modern terms, you could say they were present at every revival service Jesus ever held. They saw it all - blind eyes opening, leprous skin made whole, the paralyzed rising from their beds, demons cast out with a word, and even the dead raised to life. They didn't just hear about the power of God - they lived in it, walked in it, and watched it unfold in real time.

Yet, when the shadow of the cross fell over their hopes, when disappointment crept in and fear gripped their hearts, they forgot. Just like so many people do. We see God move, sometimes in our own lives, sometimes in the lives of those we love, and yet, when trials come or opposition rises, our memory of His miracles fade. Faith begins to leak, and fear begins to grow.

The scripture is clear: *we walk by faith, not by sight (2 Corinthians 5:7)*. As believers, we've been called to see from a higher vantage point. God doesn't view circumstances the way we do - *His ways are higher, His thoughts greater (Isaiah 55:8-9)*. But if we lack intimacy with Him, and if we don't stay close to His heart, it's easy to drift back into the realm of reason and filter our faith through experience or analytical thought. My friend, God is not meant to be figured out - He is meant to be followed.

God never asked us to put Him in a box. He never asked us to dissect Him. Every time we try to define God in human terms, we shrink His sovereignty and misrepresent His divinity.

He is not a man that He should react to circumstances. He is the Creator of all things, and His movements are intentional, eternal, and exact.

The people struggled to recognize Jesus because they expected a different kind of Messiah. For generations, they had clung to the stories of a Savior who would crush their enemies and overthrow their oppressors. They were waiting for a military champion to revolt against Rome. But instead, the Deliverer came wrapped in human weakness, born in Bethlehem, laid in a manger, and eventually nailed to a cross. They couldn't see that this humble King came not to overthrow an empire, but to overthrow sin and death itself.

Even the disciples, those closest to Jesus, missed it. In Luke, two of them walked the road to Emmaus, still dazed by the events of the crucifixion. Though they had been given the promise of a resurrected Christ and the power of the Holy Spirit, they left Jerusalem - the place where Jesus told them to wait and instead journeyed back home with hearts heavy and hope deferred. And that is exactly where Jesus met them right there on the road.

Scripture tells us they didn't recognize Him at first. As He drew near and heard their conversation, He asked what they were discussing. Their faces downcast, they told Him about how they had hoped He was the one to redeem Israel, but now He was dead, and with Him, their expectations. They recounted the crucifixion to the very One who had endured it.

But Jesus didn't scold them. He didn't rebuke them for their flickering faith. Instead, He began to remind them. He walked them through the law, the prophets, and all the scriptures that pointed to the Messiah. And as He spoke, something began to happen. Their hearts began to burn.

When they reached their home, they invited Jesus in, and here's a truth that cannot be overstated: *anytime you invite Jesus in, everything changes.* As He sat with them and broke bread, their eyes were opened. I imagine the dimly lit room, the quiet crackle of a fire, and the moment His hands lifted the bread, scarred, pierced, and marked by love. In that instant, the memory rushed back. This is my body, broken for you. And just like that, they knew. Revelation struck like lightning, and then, He vanished from their sight.

Did He disappear? Or did He simply allow Himself to be unseen? Either way, they were left with burning hearts, open eyes, and the unmistakable sound of revival ringing in their souls.

"Did not our hearts burn within us?" they exclaimed.

We know one of them was Cleopas, and scholars believe the other was Luke himself - which would make sense, since he authored this Gospel account. Regardless, what happened that day was enough to send them running back to Jerusalem, back to the upper room, back to the place of promise.

It was the fire that compelled them. A heart ignited by Jesus doesn't sit still. It's the fire of the Holy Spirit that empowers us, but it only falls in proximity to Him who is the Burning One. You cannot manufacture passion. You cannot fake spiritual fire. It is kindled in the secret place. Power does not come from performance; it comes from presence.

God is not drawn to talent; He is drawn to hunger. The angels around His throne cry *"Holy,"* but only the redeemed can sing a song the angels never will: *"Worthy is the Lamb who was slain."* There is something about the praise of a life that's walked through fire, it carries a fragrance that cannot be replicated in heaven.

Your praise moves God. The Bible says, *"He inhabits the praises of His people" (Psalm 22:3).* Small praise makes small space. Big praise makes big room. David understood this. He declared, *"I will bless the Lord at all times; His praise shall continually be in my mouth" (Psalm 34:1).* When your mouth is full of Jesus, your life will begin to reflect Him.

Psalm 34:1 NKJV - I will bless the LORD at all times; His praise shall continually be in my mouth.

This is why our focus must return to God. In today's culture, we see more performance-driven worship than true consecration. We've traded altars for stages, and presence for production. But the Church was never meant to entertain, it was meant to host the glory. It's time to give God more than two hours on a Sunday and a $20 offering. That will not sustain the fire. That will not shake a generation.

Church attendance won't break demonic strongholds. Checking a religious box won't fix spiritual battles. Going through motions won't stop a supernatural enemy. We need more than religion; we need a baptism of fire.

This generation doesn't need more information. It needs impartation. It doesn't need another polished sermon; it needs a move of God.

He is calling us deeper. He is longing for a Bride ablaze with the Spirit, empowered and purified, ready to transform cities and communities with the life, death, and resurrection power of Jesus Christ.

It's time for the hearts of God's people to burn again.

If we want revival, we must return. Return to our first love. Return to holiness. Return to hunger.

I often say this:
We need less learning, more burning.
Less thinking, more drinking.
Less debating, more demonstrating.

You were never meant to carry doubt and unbelief like a badge of survival. You were made to carry fire. And no matter what you've walked through, whether disappointment, disillusionment, or delay, God is still showing up. And when He does, He lights a match.

A House of David

They brought the Ark with joyous shouts and song,
With blood on the ground, praising and dancing strong,
The King shed his robe, humbled his pride,
And worshipped the Lord with arms open wide.

The streets were alive in a holy parade,
Trumpets rang out, thanksgiving was made.
Yet not all rejoiced in the glory that came,
One watched from the window, filled with disdain.

She mocked the King who danced without fear,
Unaware of the Glory when God draws near.
And barren she stayed; till the day she died,
A warning to those whose hearts are full of pride.

But David, he understood God's presence and grace,
It's not in a crown, but in seeking His face.
He danced, undignified, before heaven's throne,
Declaring, "The Presence of God has come home!"

Undignified.

King Saul had the crown, but David had the heart. That was the difference.

Where Saul sought position, David pursued the Presence. Saul played politics with the ark of God. He used it like a token, hoping it would guarantee him victory. But obedience mattered more than optics. Because of Saul's compromise and fear of man, the ark was lost, and with it, the presence of God left Israel. David was different.

When David became king, he had one mission: to bring the Presence back. He remembered the wilderness. It was in those hidden years tending sheep, dodging spears, and clinging to the promise of God where he learned something irreplaceable: *without God's Presence, he had nothing.*

So then, David gathered the people and tried to bring the ark home. The first attempt failed, because even passion must align with God's order. They didn't carry it the right way, and it cost the life of his friend Uzzah. So, David paused. He waited. He sought the Lord. Then came the second attempt.

This time, with reverence. Every six steps, it cost a bloody sacrifice. Every movement had to become an act of worship. It was messy and it was brutal, but it was the only way. David stripped off his royal garments and danced before the Lord in a linen ephod, celebrating like a wild man, not for attention, but because the Presence was returning.

When we finally surrender, we let go of the carefully constructed plans we built - our ideas of how life should unfold. In the light of God's wisdom, we discover that His will is revealed not through striving, but through releasing control. Performance is not promotion, and self-made stages are not the platforms heaven honors. When we stop trying to build a name for ourselves and instead make room for the Spirit of God, He does what only He can do. His way may not be the easiest path, but His Word promises us this: *"I will never leave you nor forsake you" (Deuteronomy 31:6).* That means no matter what fire we walk through, He is right there with us in it.

God does not bring you to the edge of your promise only to change His mind.

He made a covenant, a holy promise, that He would give us His Spirit. Not just to comfort us, but to teach us, guide us, and empower us to overcome every obstacle. When you are after God's heart, when you seek Him for the very direction of your calling, you can rest in this truth: He has already gone before you. He is in the middle of the warfare, and He holds the key to every victory you need.

"No weapon formed against you shall prosper" - Isaiah 54:17

I say it often, *"God has never lost a battle, and He's not about to start with yours."*

David understood something that most never will. The weight of the victory in his calling required letting go of complacency, compromise, and the need to please people. His breakthrough came when he refused to serve man's expectations and chose instead to follow God's order. When he chose to please God, he found himself truly equipped to serve God's people.

The story shifts dramatically when we see David's wife, Michal, the daughter of Saul, watching from a window. She sees David dancing wildly in His undergarments, free and undignified. She despises it. She mocks what she does not understand. But David wasn't performing for her. He wasn't dancing for applause, attention, or approval. He was worshiping the One who had chosen him.

---

2 Samuel 6:23 NLT - So Michal, the daughter of Saul, remained childless throughout her entire life.

Because Michal ridiculed what was sacred, the Bible says she remained barren for the rest of her life *(2 Samuel 6:23)*. There's a spiritual truth in that: *barren is the heart that mocks undignified worship to God. Fruitless is the life that rejects His Presence.*

But the house of David? It was blessed. His bloodline became the very lineage through which the Messiah would come. Why? Because David valued presence over popularity, sacrifice over stage, reverence over religion. David wasn't just paving the way for his own generation. He was preparing the path for every future generation - including ours. Because of one man's pursuit of the presence of God, the door was opened for all of us to dwell in the presence of God forever.

This is our generational rite of passage. Saul's era is fading. God is raising up the Davids - those who won't bow to religion, won't perform for applause, and won't bend to cultural compromise. These burning ones are marked by hunger, no matter the cost. They've walked through years in the wilderness. They've been hidden in caves, misunderstood, slandered, even violently opposed. But in those wilderness moments, they were forged by fire. They've been baptized in the flame of the Holy Spirit, and their hearts carry the wisdom of Heaven. In the secret place, God gave them a prophetic voice for cities, for regions, and for nations.

They may not look polished.
They may not sound religious.
They may even look like a bloody mess.
But these are the ones who have borne the promise in their generation. They are willing to go the distance, to pay the price, no matter how hard or how painful, because they know that to fulfill what God has called them to, it must be done God's way.

This is the call.
Will you lay down your pride and abandon performance?
Will you become undignified in worship?
Will you sacrifice comfort for revival and take back the territory the enemy tried to steal?

There will be spectators that look from the window like Michal. They'll see your praise, your tears, your fire, and they'll mock what they cannot understand. They'll say it's too messy, too radical, too much.

But understand this: *revival will not come through those who mock it from a distance.*

The Church is pregnant with the Spirit of God for a final-days awakening, and only the humble, only those willing to labor in surrender, will carry it to birth. The rest will remain spiritually barren, watching the move of God pass by through a window of religion.

It's time to open the gates.
It's time to bring the Presence home.
This is a House of David.

Forged in The Fire

They said it couldn't be, too broken to stand,
Through prayer and whispers, death close at hand.
Hell tried to claim, but Heaven broke through,
And in the darkest hour, His promise held true.

What the world saw as defeat or despair,
God was sowing fire deep in the heart of prayer.

Faith roared aloud, refusing to fall:
"Lord, if You move, Your glory will be seen by all."

Countless brushes with death,
Yet they still remained.
Not because fear was absent,
But because Heaven's purpose outlives pain.

The enemy danced, but could not hold tight,
God's Word sealed victory, turning darkness to light.

The calling was never meant to be easy,
It was born in the flames,
That brought knees to the ground
And hearts to the altar.

Now a fire burns that cannot be dimmed,
Not from trials or suffering,
But from triumph in Him.

So when you see the light shining, know this truth:
The fire did not consume,
God forged it within.

You Were Born For This.

In Acts 8, the early Church found itself in the middle of a violent storm of persecution. The disciples had seen hostility before, but this hour was unlike anything they had faced. Stephen had just been martyred, and Saul, full of rage, was ravaging the believers, tearing through homes and imprisoning followers of *The Way.*

Fear swept through the body of Christ. Every heartbeat carried the question, *"Will I live to see tomorrow?"*

But throughout history, God has proven this truth: *what looks like chaos is often the beginning of divine strategy.* What the enemy meant to crush the Church became the catalyst for its expansion.

When Luke recorded this moment in Acts, he didn't use the word "destroyed." The Greek word he used was diaspeirō - a word that means to "sow."

What appeared to be a loss to the early Church was God planting seeds of revival in new soil. What looked like people scattering was actually the gospel spreading.

Acts 8:4 GNT - The believers who were scattered went everywhere, preaching the message.

Sometimes, we cry out for deliverance from the fire when it's the fire that God is using to forge something eternal within us.

Some lives begin under the shadow of impossible odds. Others pass through moments that should have ended everything - brushes with death, danger, and devastation that leave no logical explanation for survival. Many face fires that would seem capable of extinguishing any future.

Yet none of those encounters have the final word. What God has spoken over a life cannot be silenced by diagnosis, danger, or circumstance. Because when God speaks, His word does not fade with time, it echoes into eternity.

The Bible says He knew you before you were formed in your mother's *womb (Jeremiah 1:5)*. His Word over you existed before you ever breathed your first breath. And His Word never returns void. The enemy doesn't tremble at your routine. He trembles at the resurrection Word over your life.

I once heard it said: *"The devil doesn't attack what's dead. He goes after what carries resurrection power."*

Dark valleys are not uncommon on the journey of faith. Yet it is often there - in the heat, not the highlight, that the true nature of faith is revealed. Faith is not merely quoting Scripture when the sky is blue; it is clinging to the Word when the fire rages and everything is shaking. That's the kind of faith 1 Peter 1:7 describes.

---

1 Peter 1:7 GNT - Even gold is tested by fire; and so your faith, which is much more precious than gold, must also be tested, so that it may endure.

Spiritual growth is often forged through discomfort. The stretch signals transformation. The fire marks refinement. And on the other side of every trial, the Spirit of God forges something stronger. Your faith grows into something no man can take away. True calling is not born in comfort; it is birthed in fire. And what is forged by God in the flames carries a burn that no external fire can quench.

Your current trial does not define you; it refines you. You're not being scattered. You're being sown. And the harvest that's about to come through your life will be greater than anything you've seen before.

God doesn't just want to rescue you from the fire; He wants to fill you with His Spirit so that you can walk through the fire and come out without even the smell of smoke.

"Then Nebuchadnezzar said, 'Look! I see four men walking around in the fire... and the fourth looks like a son of the gods." - Daniel 3:25

The Hebrew boys didn't bow to Babylon's idols, and they didn't burn in Babylon's flames. Instead, the fire became the stage for revival, and a pagan king declared the glory of the Living God!

Are you just performing religious rituals, or are you walking by faith and living by revelation?

Are you sitting on the sidelines of your calling, or are you stepping into the fire - trusting that God's Word over your life is still true? Let this be your moment.

No more compromise. No more complacency. No more settling for safe Christianity. You weren't made to live lukewarm. You were made to burn. God has destined you for impact, but only you can choose to step into the fire. Only you can choose to never go back. There is purpose in the struggle. There is power in your surrender.

"For such a time as this…" - Esther 4:14

Let the fire refine your faith.
Let the Word root itself deep in your spirit.
And watch as God multiplies His Kingdom through you.

Because you, my friend, are being forged in the fire.
And you were born for this.

Awakened

Awakened, cleansed by fire.
The path through the desert cannot be forced.
To wander where no eyes can see,
To find the flames that will purify fully.

Feeling the pain until nothing remains,
The end of oneself, refined by the flame.
You must choose to let everything die,
To open your soul and learn how to rise.

Hidden, forgotten, alone you may stand,
For the roots grow strongest in unknown land.
No stage, no lights, no echoing cheer,
Just stillness and trust, with God drawing near.

You must love the broken part within,
So love for others can flow from Him.
Nothing wasted, no moment lost,
Every moment of pain marked by the cross.

It is not the enemy - it is an invitation to God.
He lets the fire burn deep from within.
He leads through the desert, stripping all away,
Because only under pressure can purpose stay.

Pierced in silence, tested in dirt,
Faith is refined where flesh learns to hurt.
Alone in the fight, tested through night,
Until the stars break into morning light.

Like silver in flames, sifted and tried,
Every false idol burns from inside.
Death is shown so life is treasured,
Carrying His heart, His fire, not just His power measured.

He whispers:
"You must know who you are to love what is true.
You must learn to see Me before I send you.
I form in fire, far from human eyes,
Because I do My best work in wilderness times."

He is with you, when delay feels long,
Cloud by day, fire by night, guiding strong.
In silence and obscurity, He sharpens your sight,
Behind every closed door, He writes your name right.

He is everything, before you perform,
Before arrival, in drought and in storm.
He knows you better than your own breath,
Leading through fire, bringing life from death.

Let the wilderness do what it was made to do,
Shape something holy, deep within you.
Nothing wasted, not trial or test,
You are His beloved, and He knows what is best.

Revive: Fire & Harvest

Being born again means we're no longer who we used to be. We are made new - completely, entirely, and undeniably new. The old man is dead. The old woman is gone. The old ways of thinking, believing, and living are severed by the power of the cross.

"Therefore, if anyone is in Christ, he is a new creation. The old has passed away; behold, the new has come."
- 2 Corinthians 5:17

From the moment we are born into this world, we're shaped by its systems. We learn its limits. We absorb its patterns. We're told what's possible and what's not. But when we come to Christ, we are no longer defined by worldly standards. We are called to live by kingdom identity. The only one we're to depend on is our Father. He is our Creator. He knows us more deeply than we know ourselves. He knows our needs, our desires, our pain, and our private struggles. And He didn't just save us, He transformed us.

So now, every challenge we face must be met not as the world would, but as Jesus would.

There are moments in the journey when you can feel completely lost and convinced you have failed the call of God on your life. Circumstances can unfold in ways that leave a crushing sense of disappointment, making it seem as though you have drifted from the path He once set before you. Many have stood in that place, asking the same quiet question: *Is there a way back?*

In seasons like these, believing that things will improve can feel almost impossible. Storms have a way of clouding memory, causing the depth of God's love to fade from view. Yet the answer has never been found in the storm, it has always been found at the cross.

Jesus endured unthinkable torment knowing that humanity would still, at times, sin against Him. He was mocked, ridiculed, spat upon, and accused of being a liar even though He is Truth Himself. The Son of God was nailed to a cross He Himself had created, proving once and for all that love does not withdraw when we stumble; it remains, endures, and redeems.

"He was despised and rejected by men... pierced for our transgressions, crushed for our iniquities."- Isaiah 53:3,5

If Jesus loved us enough to die while we were still sinners *(Romans 5:8),* how much more does He love us now that we're choosing to follow Him?

There are seasons when silence lingers so long it feels as though you have been forgotten. Then, sometimes without warning, God opens a door, reminding you that He never left. Not for a single moment. He is still authoring the story, even in the quiet places. And though you may count yourself out, He never does.

Despair often takes root when the lie settles in that failure is final or defining. But failure does not define you, God does. And what He begins, He is faithful to finish.

"Being confident of this, that He who began a good work in you will carry it on to completion..."
- Philippians 1:6

The enemy will try to steal your hope, your peace, and your identity. He is a deceiver, a thief who comes to rob what God has deposited in your life. My friend, the trials you face aren't meant to destroy you. Sometimes, God allows them to refine you, strengthen you, reshape you into someone who walks with greater authority and trust.

Look at Joseph - *sold into slavery, betrayed, imprisoned, yet God raised him to govern a nation.*

Look at David - *isolated in the wilderness, hunted, forgotten, yet God anointed him king.*

Look at Elijah - *hiding in a cave, depressed, exhausted, yet God met him with a whisper.*

Seasons of isolation often become the soil where God grows the greatest fruit.

Our love for Jesus deepens when we realize how much we truly need Him. In moments of weakness, He reveals His strength. That's why we must hide His Word in our hearts, so we're not shaped by what we see but by what He says.

"Do not be conformed to this world, but be transformed by the renewing of your mind..." - Romans 12:2

"You cannot have a positive life and a negative mind."

If we want to live in the fullness of our new creation identity, it starts with renewing our minds daily and training our thoughts to agree with God's Word, not the world's voice. There will be days when it takes everything in us just to stand. But even when we don't see it, God is working.

Romans 8:28 NLT - And we know that God causes everything to work together for the good of those who love God and are called according to his purpose for them.

So stand! Truly stand. Plant your feet in the soil of His Word and refuse to be moved. Declare His promise until every lie breaks under the weight of truth. Refuse to bow to fear, to failure, and to the voice that tells you your story ends in defeat. It does not. It never has. Not when God has spoken over your life.

You were born to walk in power - His power. You were crafted for communion with the living God, not a life of mere survival or spiritual exhaustion.

You were formed to hear His voice, to carry His presence, to release His Kingdom into the very places the enemy tried to destroy you. And no matter what the enemy whispers... No matter how loud the warfare becomes... No matter how dark the night appears...

God still has a plan for your life! It's a purpose the devil cannot cancel, one the world cannot erase, one even your own past cannot disqualify.

Keep pressing. Keep trusting.

Keep leaning into the One who has never failed, never faltered, and never abandoned a single promise He has spoken.

Never forget this truth - let it burn in your bones: *You are not who you used to be.* The old you has been buried. The shame, gone. The chains, broken.

You are a new creation, awakened with resurrection breath in your lungs and destiny written on your spirit. You were reborn for a purpose far greater, deeper, and more holy than you could ever imagine.

Walk in it boldly. Heaven is waiting to back up every step you take.

"The Word of God will cut you to pieces and heal you at the same time." – Smith Wigglesworth

Rise Up

The house was still, the mourners loud,
A child lay silent, wrapped in a shroud.
Hope had fled and faith seemed thin,
They told the father, "Don't bring Him in."

But Jesus came, unmoved by fear,
He said, "She's not dead, she's only asleep here."
They laughed, they scoffed, but He closed the door,
Took her by the hand and did something more.

He spoke the words that brought back to life:
"Talitha Koum", Little girl, arise!
And breath returned where none had been,
Her soul awakened by His command.

All revered what was done,
For Jesus spoke, and death was gone.
Her parents knew He was the One.
The promised Christ, God's resurrecting Son.

Outside, the doubters and mockers missed sight,
Their unbelief in Him had veiled the light.
And in that room, where faith had tread,
He proved His power to raise the dead.

You Were Made To Rise.

In 1904, in a small town in Wales, a young man named Evan Roberts began to burn with a passion for revival. He prayed fervently for God to awaken the church. That cry sparked a move of the Holy Spirit so powerful that within months, over 100,000 people were saved. Pubs were emptied, the crime rate plummeted, and entire towns were transformed. Meetings would go all night with no preacher, just people weeping, repenting, and worshiping under the weight of God's glory. It wasn't a manufactured weekend event. It was a Spirit-breathed open portal to heaven. It wasn't revival by hype; this was revival by fire.

Do you think that 1904 was the only time that God ever wanted to release His power on the earth?

We are living in the greatest season of harvest the world has ever seen. All over the globe, the Spirit of God is pouring out. This is no longer just revival stories from the past, it's happening now. Thousands of souls are being ushered into the kingdom of God by an awakening of truth, power, and salvation. But the tragedy is that many who call themselves Christians still live like the world. Their lives carry no evidence of Jesus, no fire, no worship, and no witness. They have a form of godliness, but they deny the power that comes with it.

In Mark chapter 5 (The story of Jairus's daughter), Jesus stepped into a room filled with weeping and mockery. He wasn't concerned with the noise of culture or the religious customs of death. He saw life. He saw a miracle waiting to happen. And He knew, the child there before Him only needed to hear His voice to awaken.

"But when He had put them all outside, He took the child's father and mother and those who were with Him and entered where the child was lying." - Mark 5:40

There are moments when the Spirit of God interrupts ordinary prayer with an eternal perspective. In times of national weariness and spiritual fatigue, a single truth must be remembered: this nation is not dead. It is sleeping.

Across the world, the power of God is on display. Deaf ears open. Broken bones are healed. Demonic oppression is broken. Conditions labeled permanent are overturned by prayer. Entire communities witness the impossible. And yet, a question arises in many hearts: *Why not here? Why not now? Why does breakthrough seem delayed in certain places?*

Scripture gives insight into this tension through the story of Jairus' daughter. When Jesus arrived at the house, the atmosphere was filled with mourning, noise, and unbelief. Though He declared that the child was not dead but sleeping, the people laughed at Him. Their response revealed the condition of the room. They had made space for grief, but not for faith.

What followed is striking. Jesus removed those who refused to believe and invited only those who trusted His word to remain. Then, in the presence of faith, He awakened what appeared lifeless.

The issue was never His power. It was the atmosphere. Resurrection required room for belief.

In the same way, awakening does not come to places that declare death where God has declared life. Revival waits for hearts willing to believe again, churches willing to make room for faith, and individuals willing to stay in the room when others laugh, doubt, or walk away.

What looks like delay is often mercy. What feels like silence is often invitation. The question is not whether God still moves, but whether there is room for Him to move. And just as the story of Jairus' daughter, Jesus stands once more - this time before the sleeping church of this hour. He is not speaking over one person alone; He is speaking over a generation, calling the church to awaken, to rise, and to embrace the power and authority that has always belonged to it.

"Little girl, I say to you, arise!" - Mark 5:41

Church, wake up! Arise! It's time to shake off the grave clothes. It's time to silence the mockers and remove the doubters. It's time to get the unbelief out of the room because what God is about to do isn't for spectators or skeptics. It's for those who believe.

This is a call to refuse displacement. To stay in the room. To stand among those who believe, even when the world declares, "It's too late."

Faith still has a voice. And Jesus still raises what others have written off. In this final hour, we have to guard what we allow into our spirit. Doubt and unbelief make no room for miracles.

I'm reminded of men like John G. Lake, who would tell the sick to flush their medicine down the toilet after prayer, convinced they were healed. Or Smith Wigglesworth, who once said, *"If you pray for something seven times, you prayed six times in unbelief."* He didn't pray twice, not because he was stubborn, but because he believed that God would answer the first time. That is radical faith.

We say we have faith in God, but when prayers go unanswered, the birthplace of unbelief is conceived. And if we're not careful, we begin to make excuses for what God never intended us to accept. But the truth is, God always backs up His Word. He always fulfills His promise. He never falls asleep on His plan.

---

2 Timothy 3:1-5 ESV - But understand this, that in the last days there will come times of difficulty. For people will be lovers of self, lovers of money, proud, arrogant, abusive, disobedient to their parents, ungrateful, unholy, heartless, unappeasable, slanderous, without self-control, brutal, not loving good, treacherous, reckless, swollen with conceit, lovers of pleasure rather than lovers of God, having the appearance of godliness, but denying its power. Avoid such people.

There is a remnant rising, a people burning with fire, filled with power, and unafraid to stand in the gap. They don't live lukewarm. They don't entertain mixture. They believe the Word of God more than the report of man. They're faithful in the quiet place. They've warred in prayer when no one else was watching. And now, God is about to release a new level of authority.

The fire of God is coming to consume every trace of sickness, fear, depression, compromise, and spiritual apathy. A holy cleansing is beginning to sweep across the earth. We are standing on the edge of something the world has never seen, a move of God that will not be confined to one nation, one region, or one people.

Miracles are about to break out in ways that shake continents. Not just in foreign lands. Not just in places known for revival. Not just in the testimonies of past generations. But here. Now. In every nation hungry for His glory. From cities to villages, from crowded streets to hidden places, the Spirit of God is moving with unstoppable power.

So prepare your heart. Clear the room. Remove the mockers, the doubt, the unbelief, and the noise of the world that tries to drown out expectation.

Make space for raw, unshakable faith. Because Jesus is stepping into the room again. And when Jesus enters, the dead will rise, and hope can breathe again. Hearts become ignited and Nations awaken.

A global awakening is at the door. Get ready.

"Talitha Koum!" - Little one, I say to you - RISE UP!

The Raging Sea

They woke up to find the shore behind,
Lost at sea, with no clear line.
Waves rising high, escape feels thin,
What once was faith now pulls them in.
The cost was counted, control was laid,
The tide received what surrender gave.

But now the winds invade the chest,
And rising waters offer no rest.

One night, His presence fills the air,
A harbor formed in whispered prayer.
The next, only a windswept place,
As though He vanished without a trace.
Questions circle the turning tide:
Was something missed? Was trust denied?

His Word declares He draws near,
That storms obey when He appears.
Names are changed. The lost are found.
Yet still the waves can refuse to calm.

Transformation marks the inner core,
Though few can see what's changed for sure.
Once pain was taken from the world,
Now pain is carried for the world.
The grief runs deep, the ache feels new,
No one said revival wounds too.

They preached, "Follow and peace will stay."
But no one warned of storms this way.
No mention of waves this high,
Or nights so long they silence cries.

Did He, who faced the grave and death,
See drowning souls and choose their breath?
Does that same Spirit still remain,
When shaking comes and hope feels strained?

Old sins resurface, storms still roar,
Love is shouted, but doubt keeps score.
The soul feels wrecked, the heart feels pinned,
Faith tested by relentless wind.

Is He still near when thunder sounds?
Still an anchor when cracks abound?
Is faith still true when the pull is strong,
And tides insist you don't belong?

Religion drifts where shadows sleep,
Holy things grow dull and weak.
Yet something righteous still ignites,
A holy fire that fights the night.

And still, belief refuses to leave.
Though sails are torn and oceans grieve.
Though lightning blinds and vision bends,
The soul holds fast to what He said.

Get Out Of The Boat!

There are moments in life that feel like standing in the middle of a raging sea. The winds howl. The skies break open. The waves crash harder than expected. Prayers rise for peace, but the water keeps climbing. Hope is within reach, yet the current pulls harder still. It is in these moments that a sobering truth becomes clear: *faith is not forged on the shore - it is formed in the storm.*

It is often in these waters that the question of fairness surfaces. What does fair actually mean? Who defines it? Is fairness measured by effort, obedience, pain endured, or outcome received? Many quietly conclude that fair is simply getting what one believes is deserved.

In seasons of prolonged pressure, disappointment can harden into a single, familiar thought: *I deserve better.* It sounds reasonable. It feels justified. It often rises from real wounds, unanswered prayers, and expectations left unmet. Yet beneath that statement lies a subtle and dangerous assumption that life, God, and calling should submit to personal standards of equity.

When that belief takes root, something shifts within the soul. Entitlement begins to replace humility. Expectation replaces surrender. Instead of asking who God is forming us to become, the heart begins to measure God's goodness by comfort and outcome. And without realizing it, the soul appoints itself as judge over what better should look like.

There is a sobering truth hidden in that mindset: if life is evaluated solely through the lens of what is deserved, dissatisfaction becomes inevitable. To say I deserve better is to claim authority over the definition of better itself. And when self occupies that seat, disappointment will always follow.

Questions begin to surface. *Why would God allow this?* The storm rages within. Thoughts circle endlessly, searching for meaning, demanding fairness. This isn't right. I deserve better than this.

And there it is - the deception beneath the pain. *"I deserve better."* Entitlement disguised as disappointment. Pride hidden beneath heartbreak. The subtle belief that God has mismanaged the story.

When that lie finally is exposed, the storm breaks just enough for truth to shine through. God is revealed again, not as a negotiator of comfort, but as He truly is - sovereign, merciful, just, and good, even when life is not. His grace gives what cannot be earned. His mercy reaches deeper than the worst failure. His love pursues, even when hearts attempt to outrun it.

God's kindness is not proven by fairness. It is proven by mercy. If humanity received what it truly deserved, there would be no hope. Yet He shows compassion where judgment was due. He extends love when it is not returned. He remains faithful when faith wavers.

The storm was never meant to destroy. It was meant to reveal. Storms expose what the soul is anchored to. When faith is tied to emotion, it drifts. When hope is tethered to outcomes, it sinks. But when the soul is anchored to Christ, it stands, even in the waves.

What is needed is not a quick escape from the storm, but an anchor strong enough to withstand it.

Hebrews 6:19 NLT - This hope is a strong and trustworthy anchor for our souls. It leads us through the curtain into God's inner sanctuary.

God never promised the absence of storms. He never said the waters would always be calm. But He promised something greater: *"I will be with you."* And He is with you - in the silence, in the running, in the anger, and even in the doubt.

Striving ends, not in perfection, but in surrender. When knees hit the ground in desperation, not performance. And there, the presence of God meets the soul like the calm after a hurricane. Not with condemnation, but with remembrance. You are still His. Still called. Still loved. Still chosen.

Even when you lose sight of Him, He has never taken His eyes off you.

The enemy loves to whisper lies in the storm. He tells us that God has abandoned us, that we've failed too many times, and that the promise is over. But the storm is not the end, it's the proving ground of faith. If you'll let Him, God will meet you right in the middle of it. You don't have to wait until the skies clear to worship. You don't need perfect peace to raise your hands. You don't need to see the outcome to declare that He is good. Faith is not a feeling, it's a choice. You don't live by emotions. You live by the Word of God. You don't follow your heart. You follow His voice.

The world will tell you to trust your feelings. But feelings are like waves, ever shifting, always crashing. Faith is the anchor that holds you steady. Faith says, *"Even when I don't see it, I still believe."*

God gave us emotions, but He never intended them to define us. They are indicators, not navigators. They can help us feel, but they should never lead.

What leads is the truth of His Word.
"The just shall live by faith." - Romans 1:17
"We walk by faith, not by sight." - 2 Corinthians 5:7
"Be still and know that I am God." - Psalm 46:10

To the one reading this in a storm, let me remind you, you're not alone. God is not mad at you. He hasn't forgotten you. He sees the tears you cry in secret. He knows the war inside your heart, and He's not running from your mess. He's walking toward you in the middle of the wind and the waves, just like He did with Peter, when he was called out of the boat. *(Matthew 14)*

And just like Peter, if you start sinking, He will catch you. Don't give up. Don't go back. Don't drown in shame when Jesus already died to set you free from it. The storm may rage, but the Savior is in your boat. And when He speaks, the winds still obey. Peace is coming. Hold fast. You're going to make it through.

From Death To Glory

There was a time when a real fire fell,
When the glory of God separated Heaven from hell.
The altar blazed with holy flames,
And hearts that were touched were never the same.

But now...
I walk through sanctuaries with compromised seats,
Where entertainment and performance lead.
Songs are sung and weekly lessons taught,
But the truth of heaven doesn't pierce the heart.

Where is the glory?

The sacredness of God, sold for cheap thrills,
For instagram likes, popularity, and shallow frills.
Not truth, but fluffed up messages they speak,
Where repentance once drove every hardened heart weak.

No script, no show, no manufactured tune,
Just glory thick within the room.
We've bartered fire for fleeting fame,
Forgotten reverence of God and losing His name.

Now I wonder...
Have we surrendered holy fire for manufactured sheen?
Exchanged God's burning holiness for man's convenient
doctrine machine?
Conviction sold for popularity and crowds,
The Holy Spirit's voice drowned by the sound?

Disobedience and pride, and His glory removed.
Oh God, will you once again deliver us from evil,
Bring us back to You.

Here I Am! Send Me.

There is a story in 1 Samuel chapter 2 of a man named Eli who had 2 sons. Eli was favored by God and because of his obedience and service, he paved the way for a legacy of priesthood for his sons and the generations to come. His sons were of great stature and highly esteemed as priests. They were set apart by God and were called to steward His presence. But instead of purity, they chose perversion, and rather than offering up true sacrifice, they chose self. Scripture is brutally clear about them.

"Eli's sons were scoundrels; they had no regard for the Lord." - 1 Samuel 2:12

They stole offerings, slept with the women serving at the tabernacle, blasphemed God, and did not adhere to correction. They used their position and rank to abuse God's people. With pride and selfishness, they sought out self-indulgence, causing harm and confusion by living a life of double standards. Anytime they were confronted they shut down the opposition with force and ruled with bad intention. God warned them. He gave them time to repent, but they were driven by their own lust and pride and refused to obey. Even when God used their own father to bring correction, they refused to do it was right.

Eventually, God chose to act and bring their reign of evil to an end.

"I will raise up for Myself a faithful priest... he will walk before My anointed always." - 1 Samuel 2:35

When Eli's sons abused the holiness of God, He raised up Samuel, who since he was a young boy made the commitment to listen and obey. As he was awakened in the night by the Lord calling his name, Samuel said, *"Speak, Lord, your servant is listening."*

Samuel loved and honored God. He understood the importance of following God's order. And he also understood that doors do not stay open forever. Sometimes the call will expire if we do not answer.

God told Samuel He would do a shocking thing in Israel. The Lord explained that the sins of Eli's family would not be atoned for. A sacrifice and an offering were not going to fix things this time. Why? Because this time they had crossed a line by blatant blasphemy in the face of holiness. God had already made His decision, that the bloodline of Eli had to be killed off.

It is important to understand that if you will not be faithful to what God is telling you to do, He will raise up someone who will. That is not a threat; it's a sobering truth. God's purpose does not revolve around our preferences. He certainly isn't a God who rules as an evil dictator, forcing you to do exactly what he says.

The call of God on your life isn't about works or legalism, it is about obedience and reverence. Jesus didn't shed His blood to create a "cheap grace" generation. He gave His life to pull us out of darkness and into glory. He tore the veil so that the presence of God could touch His people once again. Too often the life of Jesus is taken for granted and narrowed down to saying a prayer so that we can live a better moral life. God isn't interested in our alter calls if it isn't leading to real born-again life transformation. He's not looking at attendance records to find out which congregation has the leading score for most alter call responses during the

Sunday service. He's not interested in boardroom meetings and blueprints to capture the attention of an audience, and heighten the need to be seen, or have the biggest following in the city. He wants hearts. He wants commitment. He wants love.

---

1 Samuel 4:21-22 NIV - She named the boy Ichabod, saying, "The Glory has departed from Israel" - because of the capture of the ark of God and the deaths of her father-in-law and her husband. She said, "The Glory has departed from Israel, for the ark of God has been captured."

That moment in Scripture is chilling. When Eli's sons led Israel into battle, they were expecting victory, but they were struck down by the Philistines. In desperation, they brought out the ark of the covenant, thinking that the presence of a sacred object would guarantee success. After all, they were of Eli's lineage, and they considered themselves to have been God's chosen ones.

As the war waged on, Israel was defeated, and thirty thousand men fell dead. The ark was captured, and the corrupt sons of Eli, Hophni and Phinehas, were killed.

This moment reveals a sobering truth: God's power cannot be manipulated. The ark without obedience is just a box, and the presence without repentance is no protection. Eli's sons were cut down, just as God had said. And a child was born into devastation - Ichabod, which translates to *"Where is the glory?"*

Where is the glory in our churches today? Where is the trembling? The repentance? The fire?

God has predestined his people to prosper and live a victorious life. Jesus didn't just come to the cross to put a stamp of approval on us so that one day we could get into heaven. His action made us right with God and made a way for us to be filled with the Holy Spirit and fire.

Let's be clear: We don't need more programs. We need the presence. We don't need better branding. We need a return to burning. We don't need louder services. We need holiness that shakes the room.

We are living in a desperate hour that needs a real move of the power of God on the Earth. My friend, there is good news. God's glory is not gone forever. It's waiting for those who will cry out, *"Show me Your glory, God!"*

2,000 years ago, the Son of God himself made a way to pour out the glory of Heaven on earth. It started in an Upper Room in Jerusalem when the fire fell. - Not religion, but power. Not ear tickling messages, but Spirit and truth that sets the captives free.

Eli's sons wanted the victory, but they didn't want the surrender. They wanted the glory of God without the weight of holiness. But the presence doesn't respond to performance, it responds to purity. The ark was never meant to be a magic weapon; it was a symbol of covenant. And God will not honor a covenant broken by pride, rebellion, or empty religion. If we want glory, we must return to the altar.

We must live the kind of lives God can trust with His presence - lives marked not by noise, but by obedience. Because glory doesn't fall on compromise. It falls on surrender.

"Speak, your servant is listening." - 1 Samuel 3:10

A Time to Kill

He was alone, with no voice, no sound,
Just canyon walls and desert ground.
A boulder pinned him where he lay,
And hope, like sun, slipped far away.

No one knew the path he took,
No rescue call, no second look.
Dreams had danced behind his eyes,
Plans and purpose now faced demise.

But then, a choice, so sharp, so clear,
Would he choose life… or disappear?

Cut it off… or die.

Aron paused with trembling breath,
Weighed the pain, the brush with death.
He didn't want to break apart,
But life still thundered in his heart.

So, with a blade and will of steel,
He made the cut that fate would seal.
He left behind what held him bound,
And walked out whole on higher ground.

For there's a time to tear away,
To leave what can't be healed or stay.
A time to kill what kills your soul,
To lose a piece… to gain the whole.

So, if you're stuck beneath regret,
Trapped by chains you won't forget,
Know this truth, harsh, yet divine:
Survival has a cost at times.

There is a time to rend, to part,
To break the grip that numbs the heart.
To choose the blade, detach, be free,
And walk into your destiny.

Kill It Before It Kills You!

In 2003, Aron Ralston, an experienced outdoorsman, went hiking alone in a remote Utah canyon. During the climb, an 800-pound boulder shifted and trapped his right arm. After being stuck for five days with no food, little water, and no hope of rescue, he made a life-or-death decision. He amputated his own arm with a dull pocketknife to survive. He walked out of the canyon missing an arm but alive.

You may never find yourself trapped under a literal boulder, but spiritually many are suffocating under the weight of sin, compromise, and comfort. The moment you were born, God had a plan for your life. It wasn't accidental or reactive. It wasn't built on your performance. It was divine, intentional, and saturated in purpose. His will is perfect, even when the journey feels anything but.

The Bible says that He knew you before you were even in your mother's womb *(Jeremiah 1:5)*. That truth from the mouth of God cancels every lie that your life is worthless. Because Jesus thought so highly of you that He paid the highest price imaginable, His very own blood.

I like to say it this way: *He thought you were to die for!*

The road to your destiny isn't easy. It's often littered with battles, distractions, challenges, and moments that make you question everything. The enemy will try to use your past, your weaknesses, and even your feelings to make you give up on what God started. But don't fall for it. The things that come against you aren't meant to destroy you; they're allowed to develop you. The very roadblocks the enemy throws in your path can become the fire that refines your character and strengthens your faith. But there's a hard truth: growth requires cutting.

We want the dream. We want the anointing. We want fire. But we don't want the knife. We want to walk into our destiny with all our habits, our pride, our bitterness, and our secret sins intact, but God's call requires a severing. The Bible puts it plainly:

Ecclesiastes 3:1-3 NIV - "There is a time to be born and a time to die... a time to kill and a time to heal."

My friend, this is a time to kill - to kill compromise, to kill the old man, and to kill the sin that's been slowly strangling your soul.

The story of Aron Ralston powerfully illustrates what so many of us refuse to do spiritually. His arm was pinned to a canyon wall. Trapped for days with no help coming and dehydration setting in, he faced a decision no one should have to make - die slowly in that canyon or cut off his own arm and live. He chose to live.

With nothing but a dull pocketknife, he cut through his own flesh and bone to free himself. It was brutal, painful, and messy, but it saved his life. And here's the reality - People are dying spiritually because they're too afraid to cut off what's killing them.

They are pinned to the canyon wall of addiction, pride, and relationships that God never blessed. With bitterness poisoning the heart, they keep praying for freedom without ever picking up the knife.

"If your right hand causes you to stumble, cut it off... it's better to lose one part than for your whole body to go to hell." - Matthew 5:30

Let that settle in... This isn't soft Christianity. This is the Gospel. It's bloody, it's messy, it's uncomfortable, but it's the cross. There are things in your life that will destroy you if you don't destroy them first. Many spend years attempting to numb deep wounds rather than allow God to heal them. Pain left untreated often seeks relief in substitutes, habits, addictions, distractions, or coping mechanisms that promise escape but quietly deepen the bondage. What begins as a mask eventually becomes a prison, eroding identity from the inside out.

Even after encountering Christ, there is a temptation to negotiate with the very things He calls us to lay down. Old patterns are managed instead of surrendered. Strongholds are tolerated instead of confronted. But freedom is never found in management, it is found in death.

The gospel does not invite you to coexist with sin. It calls you to crucify it. Revival does not come through restraint alone, but through surrender. What God exposes, He intends to heal. What He calls you to release, He plans to replace with life, power, and purity.

Freedom does not come through hiding; it comes through the cut. If destiny is to be fulfilled and purpose fully walked out, God must be allowed to perform surgery on the soul. There comes a moment when a life-changing step must be taken. It happens when you finally invite God into the hidden rooms of the heart. The masks come off. The covering ends. What remains is raw repentance.

In seasons of intentional withdrawal and surrender, the Holy Spirit goes deep. He exposes long-standing patterns - insecurities, fears, self-sabotage, and hidden sin that have ruled for far too long. And He does not merely reveal them; He cuts them away. Is it painful? Yes. Is it worth it? Eternally.

Because what is at stake isn't just your peace of mind or your ministry - it's your eternity. We must acknowledge sin to deal with it, and we must repent to obtain freedom, not just a behavior changes and not just "trying to be better." True repentance means a complete turning of direction. It is a severing. The modern church doesn't like this. It preaches seeker-friendly messages and curated Christianity. A gospel that doesn't confront sin is powerless to transform.

"If we deliberately keep on sinning... no sacrifice for sins is left." - Hebrews 10:26

If you know the truth and willingly keep going back to sin, the blood of Jesus is nullified for you. That isn't a message to scare you, it's a call to wake up. Grace isn't permission to play with sin. It's power to overcome it.

So, what's holding you back?
What keeps dragging you into the same cycles?
What keeps you spiritually pinned like Aron Ralston in that canyon?

Whatever it is, you must cut it off before it kills you.

Because one day, soon, Jesus is coming back. And He's not returning for a lukewarm church with one foot in the world. He's coming for a pure, holy, burning Bride who says, *"I will follow You, even if it costs me everything."*

This is the time to draw the sword of the Spirit. Not later. Not someday. Now. This is the moment God is calling you to stand with a holy resolve and confront everything that has been stealing your strength, draining your passion, and dulling your fire. Declare war on every thought, every relationship, every habit, and every desire that competes with Jesus.

If it lifts itself higher than His Word, tear it down. If it whispers louder than His voice, silence it. If it tries to sit on the throne of your heart, cast it out before it crowns itself king.

Tear down every idol.

Not the carved ones made of wood and stone, but the quiet ones made of comfort, pride, fear, entertainment, comparison, and self-preservation. The idols no one sees but God. The idols that slowly choke the life out of your call while pretending to be harmless.

Break every chain. Chains don't always rattle; they often disguise themselves as normal.

Routine. Patterns. "Just how I am."

But the Spirit of God will always reveal what binds you, and when He does, you don't negotiate with bondage... you break it.

Pick up the knife. The knife is surrender. The knife is obedience. The knife is the willingness to cut away what is killing your intimacy with God.

It's not gentle work. It's not comfortable. It's the holy violence Jesus spoke of when He said, "If your right hand causes you to sin, cut it off." Cut it off before it crushes your calling. Don't wait until it becomes too big to fight. Don't wait until it swallows your strength, your clarity, your joy. The things we tolerate eventually take territory, and the compromises we nurture eventually become the chains we wear.

Kill it before it kills you. Because sin never stays small. Distraction never stays harmless. Compromise never stays quiet.

What you refuse to confront will one day confront you on its own terms. But when you kill it at the root, you'll live free at the fruit. What's on the other side of the cut is resurrected life.

The moment you let the Holy Spirit separate you from what's been choking your destiny, you step into a level of freedom, clarity, purity, and authority that only comes on the other side of surrender. You discover a version of yourself you didn't know existed - a version shaped by fire, not fear... by truth, not compromise... by the Spirit, not the flesh.

This is not the hour to hesitate. This is the hour to rise. The sword is in your hand. The Spirit is within you. And resurrection is waiting on the other side of your obedience.

"The Gospel is not a discussion; it is a declaration - a sword that cuts through darkness with the fire of the Holy Spirit." – Reinhard Bonnke

The Crushing

Crushed again and again,
A reminder that we are merely men.
Prodigals wandering far from home,
Empty hearts made of dust and bone.

Lies can chain to a life despised,
Pulling you back to darkness you've tried.
So many times, to outrun, to escape,
Yet the past still haunts in shadowed shape.

You thought by now we'd rise, stand tall,
If efforts alone could fix it all.
And strength of your own could rewrite the name,
That trying harder could outrun the shame.

But the world never taught what's truly right,
Leaving broken souls alone in the night.
Hope feels distant, mercy too small,
Breathing but drifting, barely standing at all.

Wandering through darkness with no guiding light,
Every road traveled leads deeper out of sight.
The world needed a Savior, One who could pay the price,
For souls that were drowning in wounds, consequences,
and vice.

My friend Jesus loves you, I know you may not see how,
When shame wraps tight and the heart is a shroud.
When freedom feels distant, and truth just a spark,
Where pain has been constant and darkness left its mark.

Life without Jesus is a war with no end,
A storm with no shelter, a foe you cannot bend.
A soul unrefined is barely alive,
Running through shadows with no strength to survive.

Yet the place where breaking begins
is the place mercy wakes,
Where fire meets flesh and truth overtakes.
Like Joseph in prison, like David in caves,
God refines deeply through trials and waves.

You feel the breaking, the tearing away,
A furnace of trials, a wilderness stay.
Like olives in pressing, like gold in the flame,
Chains are stripped until nothing remains.

Thank God for the crushing, for mercy that frees,
For the blood of the Lamb breaking all curses and lies.
The nails in His hands pierce shadows and sin,
Flooding the darkness and letting light in.

Battered, misused, bruised, and worn,
Surrender becomes the seed where strength is born.
In giving Him nothing, He gives everything,
Turning every crushing into a holy refining.

How much more can a soul truly take?
Every breaking is heaven remaking.
Every pressure a promise, every tear a seed,
For the oil of His anointing flows from need.

God uproots falsehood, tears down pride,
Crushing what kills the people inside.

One truth remains for all who choose Him:
Following Jesus is stepping into fire,
A holy flame burning all He never desired.

It scorches the false, refines what remains,
And once you follow Him, nothing stays the same.

Purpose In The Pain.

There comes a point in every believer's story when the poetry on the page becomes the process of the soul. Crushing is not a punishment; it is a refining. It is the holy pressure where the old life dies, and the resurrected life begins. Every burning one must pass through it. Every disciple must face it. Every revivalist has been forged by it.

But here is the truth the enemy never wants you to realize:
You are not crushed to be destroyed.
You are crushed to be poured out.
You are crushed to be made new.

Just as olives release oil only when pressed, and grapes empty their sweetness only when crushed, the Spirit produces anointing through the places where life tries to break you. This is not just your story; it's the story of Scripture from beginning to end.

Moses was crushed in the desert.
Joseph was crushed in the pit.
David was crushed in the cave.
Elijah was crushed under the broom tree.
Peter was crushed by his denial.
Even Jesus Himself was crushed in Gethsemane.

Crushing is the birthplace of calling.

And it is in the crushing that your eyes are finally opened to a deeper truth – a truth that believers often wrestle with: *You cannot clean yourself up to come to Jesus. You come to Jesus, and He cleanses you.*

The Crushing of Misunderstanding

Many spend years wrestling inwardly, believing they must become worthy before drawing near to God. Familiar language about salvation may be learned early, yet the burden of transformation can feel as though it rests on human effort alone. From that place, lies take root: *I'm too dirty for Him. I need to fix myself first. I can't come to Jesus until I'm better.* But these thoughts do not come from grace, they come from misunderstanding it.

Grace does not wait for you to be clean; it is what makes you clean. Transformation is not the price of proximity to God - it is the result of it.

***"While we were still sinners, Christ died for us."* - Romans 5:8**

You don't get clean and then come to Him. You come to Him, and He makes you clean.

Scripture gives one of the most powerful pictures of this in Luke 5:12-14.

Luke 5:12-14 NLT - In one of the villages, Jesus met a man with an advanced case of leprosy. When the man saw Jesus, he bowed with his face to the ground, begging to be healed. "Lord," he said, "if you are willing, you can heal me and make me clean." Jesus reached out and touched him. "I am willing," he said.

"Be healed!" And instantly the leprosy disappeared. Then Jesus instructed him not to tell anyone what had happened. He said, "Go to the priest and let him examine you. Take along the offering required in the law of Moses for those who have been healed of leprosy. This will be a public testimony that you have been cleansed."

Jesus touches the untouchable. People with leprosy in biblical times lived in isolation - cut off, unclean, and rejected. They were the forgotten ones, the ones society pushed out, and religion gave up on them. Under the old covenant, touching the unclean made you unclean.

But watch what Jesus does. He reaches out His hand and touches the man no one would touch. In that single moment, Jesus did the unthinkable. He broke the barrier of shame. He overturned religious fear. He rewrote the rules of clean and unclean.

In the old way, the unclean contaminated the clean, but in the new way, the Clean One made the unclean clean. The touch of Jesus does not contaminate, it transforms. That's why He could declare to the person with leprosy, *"I am willing. Be cleansed" (Luke 5:13)*.
And that same voice speaks over you, over your story, and over your crushing - *"I am willing. Be cleansed."*

The Crushing of Religion

Have you ever felt unworthy, too messy, too broken – like you came out of one form of bondage only to step into another? Religion can be a system heavy on performance but light on true transformation. A family meant to nurture can become a structure that confines. A bride meant to burn with Spirit-led passion can be treated as a business model. A culture meant to embrace grace can demand perfection.

That dissonance can crush the soul, but even in the weight of it, there is mercy. For God uses the breaking of the false to reveal the real, uprooting what is hollow to make room for what is alive.

You weren't meant to live under the weight of performance. You were meant to live under the power of the cross. Charles Spurgeon said: *"I have learned to kiss the waves that throw me against the Rock of Ages."*

Every wave of misunderstanding, every crushing of expectation, and every storm of religion was meant to push you deeper into Jesus.

The Crushing of Transformation

This world needs a real Savior, a real Deliverer with real power, not a polished system but a consuming fire. And the only way to walk in that fire is to surrender everything that dulls its flame. Crushing teaches surrender, surrender breaks pride, and broken pride births true freedom.

These are the prayers hell hates - *"God, take the world out of me"*, *"Cut away everything that doesn't look like You"*, and *"Shake me until nothing remains but holiness."*

Those are dangerous prayers - not because God is cruel, but because He loves you too much to leave you unchanged. Crushing is not God's anger. Crushing is God's craftsmanship. He prunes to heal. He presses to purify. He stretches to strengthen. He breaks to rebuild. And He romances your spirit through every painful inch of it, drawing you into a love deeper than fear, a faith stronger than storms, and a purity forged by fire.

The Promise in the Crushing
Here is the revelation every believer must carry - The crushing is not the end. It is the formation of the vessel. It is the oil behind the anointing. It is the fire behind the calling. When you feel like you can't take any more, that is the moment Heaven pours more grace. When the weight feels unbearable, that is the moment God strengthens your frame.

When the crushing feels endless, that is the moment resurrection begins. A.W. Tozer said: *"It is doubtful whether God can bless a man greatly until He has hurt him deeply."*

The hurt is holy, the crushing is sacred, and the outcome is glorious. Because the crushing does not break you, it reveals you.

Breathe

The pressure closes in like flames on the chest,
Not to destroy, but to prove what is best.
Every step that is taken, every breath that is claimed,
Burns away the smoke that hides from His name.

It isn't falling, it's learning to fight,
Between what was broken and what burns with light.
Rejection may choke you, disappointment may bind,
But the fire forms a crown for the steadfast mind.

The sting of failure will come, that is true,
The weight of mistakes tries to bury you.
Yet this is the fire that refines and restores,
Turning ashes to gold, breaking old doors.

Even when night seems endless, and the waves rise high,
Even when hope feels lost and the soul wants to cry,
Remember the One who breathed beyond pain,
The One who still rises and breaks every chain.

So stand in the fire, let it sharpen the flame,
Not seeking escape, not playing the game.
Every trial is a forge, every crushing a test,
Every pressure a promise to bring out the best.

Old cycles fall like embers to ground,
Every lie is silenced where victory is found.
Fear is expelled, doubt swept away,
Faith ignites stronger with each passing day.

Breathe in the fire, let it scorch what is false,
Let it burn away pride; let it refine every pulse.
Rise from the ashes, take hold of the call,
Nothing survives the fire that God uses for all.

This is the hour, the moment, the fight,
Step into the flames, let the fire be your light.
Stand where the world would tell you to flee,
And rise in the blaze of eternity.

Joy Comes In The Morning.

A life with God is not a casual agreement, it is a covenant of fire.

When you say yes to Him, you are saying no to everything that once controlled you. You're stepping into a holy war between your old nature and the new creation He is forming inside you. All the old desires of the flesh must die, and like any real relationship, it demands loyalty, pursuit, and affection pointed in one direction - toward Him and Him alone.

If you think about it from a marital perspective, the picture becomes even more clear. A marriage where only one person is committed is not marriage, it's misery. No one would celebrate a covenant where one spouse keeps affection for other lovers. No one would enter a union where the other party only shows up once a week. The relationship we have with God is the same. He is not interested in part-time affection. He wants a burning, wholehearted devotion.

"You can't be the bride of Christ while remaining a harlot to the world."

When Christ saves us, our desires must shift, and our affections must be purified. Love for God looks like loyalty to God. It looks like laying down anything that tries to compete with Him. Faithfulness is not legalism, it's love.

When we face crucial moments in life, there is a decision to be made that feels like the crossroads of destiny. Will you keep your eyes locked on Jesus, or turn and run under the weight of failure?

Before salvation, our lives are marked by choices that wound others deeply. Lies are spoken. Trust is broken. Manipulation, betrayal, and theft leave consequences that ripple outward like shockwaves, touching everyone close enough to feel the impact.

Some respond with rejection. Others with disappointment. And even after repentance, after crying out to God, the memories do not always disappear overnight. Guilt can tighten like chains. Shame can press into the chest like thorns. Pain can become embedded in the heart - something carried everywhere, even into new seasons. And sometimes, even when forgiveness is offered by those who were hurt, the hardest forgiveness to receive is your own.

This is the place where the mind becomes the battlefield, where every breath feels trapped beneath the weight of condemnation, and when the enemy whispers that rising again is no longer possible.

Trauma does not vanish on command. The fallout of sin often extends far beyond the moment it occurred, and more often than not, the last person to receive healing is the one carrying the deepest shame.

There are days that feel normal. And then there are days when life seems to be pulled from the lungs - when breathing feels laborious and when the pain is not physical but spiritual. It's like suffocating heaviness born from the aftermath of past choices. It can feel like drowning in what has already been forgiven yet not fully healed.

Proverbs 4:23 NKJV - Keep your heart with all diligence, for out of it spring the issues of life.

What's inside your heart decides the rhythm of your life. When guilt, shame, and condemnation settle there, they choke out joy, peace, and spiritual breath. God warns us to guard our hearts, not because He wants to control us, but because He knows that sin suffocates. Compromise constricts. Hidden wounds steal oxygen from our spirit.

And here's the truth the enemy never wants you to realize: *God does not use shame to change you, He uses fire.* His fire doesn't suffocate; it purifies. His fire doesn't punish; it frees. His fire doesn't destroy the child; it destroys the chains.

Satan knows your weaknesses, and he will always use them to provoke you, distract you, and pull your eyes off Jesus. If you play with sin, it will take over. If you feed the flesh, it will dominate you, but if you resist the enemy, if you stay in prayer, if you stay in the Word, God gives you the supernatural strength to overcome what once overcame you.

Healing from guilt and shame does not happen overnight. It takes time, wrestling, tears, and the deliberate choice to refuse surrender to despair. Slowly, through the relentless love of God, something begins to shift. The grip of grief loosens. The suffocating weight begins to lift. Breath returns to the soul.

This is not the end. It is refinement. God uses the fire to burn away everything that is not Him, leaving behind what is true, purified, and eternal.

Sometimes the fire hurts because it removes what we were never meant to carry.

Somebody reading this has been living in a cycle of regret, secrecy, and pain. A cycle of suffocating under the weight of your past.

But hear me - Cycles break where surrender begins. Bondage snaps where humility meets the power of God. Shame loses its voice when you finally breathe out what you've been holding in. If it's a secret sin, He can free you. If it's addiction, He can break it. If it's anger, He can heal it. If it's heartbreak, He can restore it. If it's spiritual depletion, He can breathe life back into your lungs.

Maybe you're reading this with tears in your eyes because you know exactly what it's like to feel spiritually winded. Like no matter how hard you try, you can't get full breath.
Like the weight of your decisions sits on your chest every morning. God sees you. God hears you. God has not abandoned you in the fire. He is the One standing in it with you.

If you're ready to breathe again, if you're ready to step out of guilt and into grace, and if you're ready to let the fire refine you rather than consume you…

Say this prayer - *"Lord, I come to You in humility. I recognize You as the God of the universe. I believe in You, and I believe that You love me. Thank You Jesus, for giving Your life for me. I cannot carry this pain any longer, and I can't breathe under the weight of my mistakes. I need You, Jesus.*

Please forgive me for my actions and forgive me for sinning against you. I repent. Wash me and make me whole again. I release it all to you. Help me breathe again. Become the Lord of my life and show me how to make amends with those I've hurt. Fill me with your Holy Spirit and lead me in strength and courage to live a holy life. In Jesus' name… Amen."

Take Up Your Cross

His Word speaks of mercy and release,
Yet lives still interrogate what forgiveness means.
Declarations made, then broken again,
Hands reaching heaven, retreating in shame.

Beneath wide skies and unblinking stars,
Questions arise from men's wounded hearts.
Does He still care when the burden is grave,
When the weight feels heavier than strength can bear?

There may be days when the soul feels whole,
Before drifting far from the center and call.
Identity formed, then quietly frayed,
The former self can slowly start to fade.

When prayers are lifted for others in need,
Hope is awakened by miracles seen.
The wilderness can still claim its ground,
Where faith feels thin and hope feels bound.

Where the mind insists that He is near and true,
and silence lingers the whole night through.
Unspoken questions can surface again:
Forgotten? Misplaced? A flaw in the plan?

Still, something remains that refuses retreat,
Even when standing in fire and defeat.
For walking away would demand a cost
Far greater than pain, far deeper than loss.

Grace is longed for but cannot be earned,
No strength sufficient, no lesson learned.
Mercy is not a measured reward,
Nor weighed by failure or effort poured.

The wound runs deep, unseen, unheard,
Yet joy still stirs beneath the hurt.
Pain will not have the final word,
Morning is promised, though distant and blurred.

Memory returns to Gethsemane's ground,
Where Jesus knelt with no one around.
He felt the sorrow, counted the cost,
Yet chose the cross and refused the loss.

This is the call that few will choose:
To carry the cross when the night won't move.
To endure the fire, remain in the flame,
Trusting the dawn will still bear His name.

So rising comes on trembling ground,
Hearts still aching, faith still wound.
The road is hard, but one truth stays:
Turning back demands a higher price.

Bruised, but not finished. Worn, but alive.
The night will not win; the dawn will arrive.
And even here, when strength feels thin,
The choice remains, to choose Him again.

Who Do You Say I Am?

In the garden of Gethsemane, we see one of the most sobering moments in Scripture. Jesus, fully God yet fully human, entered the deepest anguish. He knew the weight of what was coming - the betrayal, the suffering, the cross. Scripture says His soul was *"deeply grieved to the point of death."*

Then Jesus came with them to a place called Gethsemane, and told His disciples, "Sit here while I go over there and pray." And He took Peter and the two sons of Zebedee with Him and began to be grieved and distressed. Then He said to them, "My soul is deeply grieved, to the point of death; remain here and keep watch with Me."

And He went a little beyond them, and fell on His face and prayed, saying, "My Father, if it is possible, let this cup pass from Me; yet not as I will, but as You will." And He came to the disciples and found them sleeping, and He said to Peter, "So, you men could not keep watch with Me for one hour? Keep watching and praying, so that you do not come into temptation; the spirit is willing, but the flesh is weak."

He went away again a second time and prayed, saying, "My Father, if this cup cannot pass away unless I drink from it, Your will be done." Again, He came and found them sleeping, for their eyes were heavy. And He left them again, and went away and prayed a third time, saying the same thing once more.

Then He came to the disciples and said to them, "Are you still sleeping and resting? Behold, the hour is at hand, and the Son of Man is being betrayed into the hands of sinners. Get up, let's go; behold, the one who is betraying Me is near!" - Matthew 26:36-46

Here we see the Son of God - holy, pure, fully divine yet wrapped in fragile flesh. He was entering the deepest anguish any human heart has ever known. He knew the weight of the sacrifice before Him. He knew the sting of betrayal. He knew the agony of the cross long before a nail ever pierced His body. Scripture says His soul was *"deeply grieved to the point of death."* This wasn't a moment of weakness. It was a moment of warfare, of will, and of surrender. It was the place where the humanity of Jesus met the holiness of obedience.

Jesus felt emotions as you do. He faced temptation as you do. He felt the crushing weight of what obedience would cost. And yet, He never allowed emotions to dictate His obedience. He never allowed fear to silence His calling. He never allowed the desire to escape to redirect His destiny.

He poured out His heart before the Father with honesty, vulnerability, and holy reverence saying, *"If there is any other way … yet not My will, but Yours."*

Even in His trembling, He did not waver. Even in His anguish, He obeyed. Even in His suffering, He surrendered. Jesus modeled the deepest truth of the Kingdom: *Surrender is not defeat; it is victory.*

Anguish is not foreign to the human soul. There are moments when loneliness clings like a shadow that will not lift - when obscurity, rejection, and perceived failure press so heavily that it feels as though your very identity is being crushed. You may feel bare. Exposed. Unseen. Unwanted.

Yet even in that valley, there is often a whisper, not one that shouts or demands, but one that simply says, "I am still here."

How much easier it would be if Jesus appeared again in the flesh, if faith could point to something tangible, something visible. But this is the narrow road faith walks: trusting when your eyes see nothing, trusting when your heart feels nothing, and trusting when the ground beneath you shakes. And still, the beauty remains, no matter what you cannot see or feel, His promise stands unmoved.

There comes a revelation that reshapes everything: *God's presence is not proven by your comfort, but by His covenant.*

At some point, a choice must be made. A holy resolve forms in the heart that says, If You are not leaving me, then I will not leave You. And in that surrender, something breaks, not in God, but within you. Pride begins to die. Illusions fall away. The need for control loosens its grip.

From that grave rises a deeper faith - pure, surrendered, and refined by fire. Because faith is not born in comfort; it is born in conflict. Its foundation is not laid upon blessings, but upon surrender.

Joshua 1:9 NLT - This is my command - be strong and courageous! Do not be afraid or discouraged. For the LORD your God is with you wherever you go.

God commands His people continually to be strong and courageous. Not because courage comes naturally, but because courage must often be chosen while fear still whispers. Sometimes courage looks like slaying giants. But more often, courage looks like standing still. Standing firm. Standing when everything in you wants to run. Standing when doubt screams louder than faith. Standing when your flesh tries to convince you that comfort is safer than surrender. Sometimes courage is not the roar of a lion, but the quiet resolve of a heart that refuses to bow.

In Matthew Chapter 26, Jesus asked His disciples to stay awake with Him, but they fell asleep. He asked for their presence; they chose their comfort. He asked them to watch and pray; they chose rest over responsibility. And how often do we do the same? How often do we silence conviction because convenience speaks louder? How often do we ignore the invitation to pray because entertainment is easier? How often do we choose to sleep when Heaven is asking us to watch and war?

To follow Jesus is to take up a cross. It is to lay down your will for His will. It is to die to unrighteousness so His righteousness may live through you. This kind of surrender is painful. It strips of you. It empties you. It confronts the parts of you that still crave control. But it is in that death that resurrection power is found. Even Jesus cried out for another way. Yet for the joy set before Him, He endured the cross. You were that joy. *(Hebrews 12:2)*

When Christ becomes your joy, your reason, your treasure, and your pursuit, no cost becomes too great. We must stop living as though Jesus came to enhance our life. He came to be our life. It is not Jesus plus your dreams. Not Jesus plus your preferences. Not Jesus plus your comfort. It is

Christ your life - your purpose, your identity, and your everything.

When you meet Jesus, everything changes. Your desires shift. Your addictions break. Your priorities re-align. Your heart awakens. Many people say they are Christians, but their lives mirror the world. They claim Him with their lips but deny Him with their lifestyle. They want salvation without surrender, blessing without obedience, resurrection without a cross. But Jesus paid for more than church attendance. He paid for transformation. He paid for holiness. He paid for freedom.

If you are in darkness, He is the light. If you are oppressed, His blood has already purchased your liberty. If you are bound by fear, His cross has already broken its hold.

Every trial, every fire, every valley has one purpose - to reveal the authenticity of your faith.

Jesus asked His disciples a question that still confronts every human heart today - *"Who do you say I am?"*
He didn't ask, "Who do your parents say He is? Who does the church say He is? Who does culture say He is?

Is He Lord of your life, or merely a comforting thought?
Is He Master, or a motivational idea?
Is He King, or a convenient addition to you?

When Jesus rebuked Peter, He exposed the battle we all face - the temptation to see life through the lens of our desires rather than the perspective of God. The cross cannot be skipped. It cannot be softened. There is no Christianity without crucifixion. There is no discipleship without denial. To follow Him is to die. To die is to live.

What is the Holy Spirit asking you to lay down? What part of you must die so Christ can live through you? What sin, habit, entitlement, relationship, dream, or desire is competing for the throne of your heart?

In the wilderness, Jesus was offered shortcuts - promises without a cross, power without obedience, identity without intimacy. But He chose the cross. And so must we.

Our choice is either faith or fear, the cross or compromise, and obedience or disobedience. And at the end of it all, one question remains - the question Heaven will ask you; the question eternity hinges on...

Who do you say He is?

Slaying Giants

Giants still rise, not only in ancient tales,
But in valleys where destiny is weighed on scales.
They thunder threats, demand retreat,
Commanding fear to bow in defeat.
Yet faith still answers, clear and loud:
Arise. Advance. Don't bow to doubt.

There are seasons when courage seems thin,
When promise glows but strength wears dim.
The cost feels heavy, the odds too steep,
And waiting feels safer than the leap.

So often the land lies just ahead,
Yet fear is crowned inside the head.
The fruit is near, the promise plain,
But giant voices rule the terrain.

Fear speaks first and claims the ground,
Till heaven's voice breaks through the sound,
Not soft, not weak, not filled with delay,
But fire declaring: Move today.

Be strong. Be brave. Do not withdraw.
The victory comes by the Spirit's power.
The line is drawn. The moment stands.
Possession waits for obedient hands.

Not by human strength or sharpened steel,
But by the Spirit victory is sealed.
When faith advances, lines are crossed,
And giants fall at heaven's cost.

No battle is faced by flesh alone.
Fire from heaven meets flesh and bone.
The war is real, the ground is torn,
But obedience is where triumph is born.

Victory lives where faith stands tall,
Where vision rises beyond the wall.
The promised land is never seized
By hearts that tremble, stall, or freeze.

It is claimed by those who choose to stay
When pressure screams, Turn back. Delay.
By burning ones who move in trust
While everything demands the dust.

The hour stands. The call is clear.
This is the moment marked in fear.
Every lie the enemy framed
Falls beneath Jesus' name.

Giants tremble when saints advance.
Heaven moves when faith takes stance.
The Kingdom comes where ground is found,
And every giant bows to sound.

Fearless And Full Of Faith.

There's a vast difference between hearing about victory and walking in it. People admire victory from a distance, talk about it, preach about it, sing about it... but few step into it.

The Israelites were no strangers to miracles. They had watched the Red Sea peel open like curtains at God's command. They tasted manna that fell from heaven every single morning. They drank water that poured from a rock in the desert. They were surrounded and saturated by the supernatural. Yet when they stood at the threshold of promise - they froze. Not because the giants were stronger, but because their belief was weaker. Out of the 12 spies that were sent into the promised land to scout it out, only 2 were unafraid.

Numbers 13 tells us the majority saw themselves as grasshoppers. Not because they were, but because they believed they were.

Numbers 13:33 NLT - "We seemed like grasshoppers in our own eyes, and we looked the same to them."

That's the devastating power of belief: *the way you see yourself decides the way you face your giants.* If you see through the eyes of fear, you'll shrink back. But if you see through the eyes of faith, you'll step forward. Joshua and Caleb stood in the same place, saw the same giants, breathed the same air, but carried a different spirit. Ten of the spies who were sent to scout the land saw death; two saw their destiny. Where the others saw obstacles, Joshua and Caleb saw opportunity. Their hearts were anchored in the faithfulness of the God who had already proven Himself repeatedly.

And years later, when Joshua took the lead, he didn't hesitate, bargain, or negotiate.
He walked boldly into the land with a prophetic word roaring inside him.

"Be strong and courageous! Do not be afraid or discouraged. For the Lord your God is with you wherever you go." - Joshua 1:9

This wasn't God's suggestion. It was His command. Courage is not the absence of fear; it's the refusal to bow to it. Faith doesn't deny the existence of giants; faith simply denies them authority. A teenage boy named David understood that. When he faced the Philistine giant in battle, he knew he didn't match Goliath's strength. Yet, he didn't need armor, approval, or applause. He didn't negotiate with the giant. He declared victory before the stone ever flew because faith always speaks from heaven's perspective.

Faith doesn't react, faith prophesies. Faith doesn't run; it conquers.

As revivalist William Newton Clarke once said, *"Faith is the daring of the soul to go farther than it can see."*

You may be facing a giant right now - financial lack, sickness, fear, addiction, rejection, or doubt. The wilderness has a way of squeezing us until everything buried beneath the surface is forced into the light. It exposes fear so courage can rise. Your greatest weapon is not strategy, money, or charisma, it is faith and obedience to the call of God on your life.

Here's what Israel never realized - while they wandered in circles, while they cried, questioned, doubted, and hesitated, their enemies were already terrified of them. Rahab revealed the truth.

"We are all afraid of you... No one has the courage to fight you... For the Lord your God is the supreme God."
- Joshua 2:9–11

That revelation changes everything. The giant you fear may already be trembling at the sound of your name. Hell recognizes those who carry heaven's authority, even when you don't.

Leonard Ravenhill declared, *"The world is not waiting for a new definition of Christianity, but a new demonstration of it."*

And God is raising a generation that will prove, not just discuss, debate, or describe the Kingdom of God with fire. You were not created to retreat at the sight of opposition. You were created to rule, reign, and advance the Kingdom with boldness. Jesus Himself said, *"Behold, I give you authority to tread on serpents and scorpions, and over all the power of the enemy; and nothing shall harm you." - Luke 10:19 KJV*

When you know who walks before you, fear loses its grip. The cross didn't leave the victory unfinished, it sealed it.

Sometimes doubt still clings to us. Sometimes the voices of people echo louder than the voice of God. Sometimes the wilderness feels like abandonment. But the wilderness is not your grave, it is your training ground. It is the place where God strips away fear, and forges warriors. Hudson Taylor said it beautifully - *"God is not looking for extraordinary people, but for ordinary people who will trust an extraordinary God."*

Every trial calls you deeper. Every obstacle strengthens your resolve. Every roar of every giant is an invitation for faith to roar louder. So, rise-up warrior! You were created for this moment. You were born for battlefields, not comfort zones. Stop running from what you were anointed to conquer. Stop bowing to fear that has already been defeated. Stop believing the lies of the enemy when God's Word is louder.

You carry the Spirit that raised Jesus from the dead. The same Spirit that turns ordinary disciples into bold revivalists. The same Spirit that empowers frail humanity to do impossible things. Don't just believe the promise, own it. Don't just sing about victory, walk in it.

You were never meant to run from giants. You were born to slay them!

"When the Spirit of God comes upon a man, he becomes more than human - he becomes a flame, a living sword in the hand of God." – John G. Lake

The Hour For Rain

Upon the mountain, bold and clear,
A lone prophet faced the crowd without fear.
The prophets cried to Baal in vain,
Their prayers unanswered, no fire, no flame.

Elijah stood, voice strong, profound,
And called on God, His Name renowned.
The altar blazing, wood soaked through,
Fire fell and showed God's power true.

The people watched, their hearts awake,
The false prophets' claims began to break.
One by one, they fell to the sword,
Their lies exposed, their glory ignored.

Then Elijah turned, the work not done,
He prayed for rain beneath the sun.
The sky remained clear, the heavens still,
Yet His faith within obeyed God's will.

No eye could see, no voice could part,
The clouds that formed within his heart.
A whisper first, then growing sound,
A storm of mercy on dry ground.

Though scoffers laughed, though doubts were spread,
He spoke what only heaven had said:
"Make ready now, for rain will fall!"
And faith endured above it all.

For when God moves, the world may jeer,
But fire and rain will both appear.
So stand in faith, declare His Name,
Revival fire is coming, now let it rain!

Here Comes The Rain.

There can be seasons in life when everything feels dry. It is these moments when it feels like our prayers have gone unheard and the promises of God feel delayed. The spiritual atmosphere can feel heavy, stagnant, and almost suffocating. It's the kind of dryness that makes a person wonder, *"God, where are You in all of this?"* But dryness is never absence, silence is never abandonment, and delay is never denial.

God is the God who works behind the scenes - in the hidden, the unseen, the quiet, and the waiting. He is moving even when the land of our soul feels barren and the heavens feel shut. Elijah knew that feeling well.

Scripture tells us that for three and a half years *(Luke 4:25, James 5:17),* there was no rain in Israel. The drought was both natural and spiritual. The skies had dried up, but worse, the hearts of the people had dried up. Israel had turned to Baal, seduced by idolatry, compromising their worship, their purity, and their covenant with God.

But when God wants to restore a nation, He raises a voice. He raises a prophet - a revivalist – a fire starter. And so, God sent Elijah to confront not just a weather system, but a spiritual system. Elijah's showdown on Mount Carmel wasn't just a miracle moment; it was a national turning point. He rebuilt the broken altar of the Lord, stone by stone, because before revival hits a nation, revival must first rebuild the altar.

And when Elijah prayed, God answered with fire! A fire that consumed the sacrifice,
the wood, the stones, the water, and the dust beneath their feet *(1 Kings 18:38)*. God's fire silenced every false god, and it made the entire nation cry out, *"The Lord, He is God! The Lord, He is God!" - 1 Kings 18:39*

But there is something people tend to overlook - *The fire was only the beginning.* The fire broke deception but the rain would break the drought. Revival always begins with fire, but it is sustained by rain.

After the fire, Elijah didn't relax. He didn't celebrate prematurely. He didn't say, *"Well, that's enough for today."* He climbed higher. He bowed lower. He pressed deeper. Then he declared a prophetic word that made no logical sense*, "I hear the sound of abundance of rain." - 1 Kings 18:41*

There were no clouds in the sky, no thunder, no moisture, not even a breeze. Yet Elijah heard what heaven was preparing. This is the essence of revival faith: *hearing the rain before the sky darkens.*

Elijah sent his servant to look not once, but seven times. Six times the servant saw nothing. Six times the sky mocked the promise. Six times faith was tested. But on the seventh time, the number of completion, he saw it. There was a cloud the size of a man's hand rising from the sea. Though it seemed small, insignificant, and barely visible, it was enough to ignite the faith in Elijah. A move from Heaven often begins with something small - a whisper, a stirring, a remnant, maybe even a single spark. Elijah knew: *"That's it. That's the beginning of the downpour."*

We often imagine prophets as fearless, unshakable giants, but Scripture shows us Elijah was painfully human. He confronted kings, false prophets, and idol worshipers, but he also battled loneliness, fear, and even depression *(1 Kings 19).* Faith does not end human emotion, faith overrules it.

Elijah carried the burden of revival on his back. He stood alone against 450 prophets of Baal and an entire nation in compromise. He risked his life every time he spoke the Word of the Lord. But God had positioned him exactly where he needed to be, at exactly the right time.

Revival requires voices who won't back down. Revival requires people who will rebuild what others let fall. Revival requires intercessors who will pray until rain breaks the drought. Revival requires faith that will keep climbing the mountain even when the sky stays clear. This is the call for us today - When you stand in righteousness, when you choose holiness, and when you walk in obedience you carry heaven's authority on earth. Opposition will rise. Mocking voices will echo. Doubt will whisper. Warfare will intensify. But the promises of God never fail.

The same God who dropped fire from heaven and sent rain over a drought-stricken land, is the same God working in your life, your ministry, your calling, your family, and your generation. Your prayers matter. Your declarations shift atmospheres. Your faith moves mountains. Your worship changes climates. Heaven is waiting for Elijah-like believers who refuse to bow to dry seasons.

The moment the rain came, everything transformed. The soil softened, the fields revived, and God's people were renewed. Their hearts were awakened to truth, and the once lost hope was resurrected. Because Elijah stood boldly in the face of compromise, faith blossomed again.

This is how revival unfolds. It is a fire in the heart, a downpour of rain in a weary land. First, God sets a soul ablaze. Then He pours out His Spirit on everything around it.

Even now, we are living in a prophetic moment. Across the globe in nations, cities, and tribes revival fires are burning. Souls are being saved in unprecedented numbers. The Spirit of God is moving in ways we've never seen before.

We are in the early rumblings of the last-days outpouring Joel prophesied *(Joel 2:28–29)*. We may not see the full storm yet, but there is a cloud rising on the horizon. We can feel the shift. We can sense the urgency. We can hear the sound. And in this hour, just like Elijah, we declare the promise before it manifests: *"Let it rain!"*

Stand firm. Pray boldly. Walk in holiness. Prophesy the promise. Refuse to bow to dry seasons. Because the rain is coming - the rain of revival, the rain of awakening, and the rain that will saturate a generation and prepare the earth for the return of the King.

The fire has fallen.
Now it's time for the rain.

---

1 Kings 18:41 NLT - Then Elijah said to Ahab, "Go get something to eat and drink, for I hear a mighty rainstorm coming!"

Eyes Like Fire, Sword in Mouth

He comes not clothed in silence,
But robed in glory bright,
With eyes that burn with a holy flame,
And pierce the darkest night.

No shadow hides before Him,
No heart escapes His gaze,
He sees through every compromise,
And sets the soul ablaze.

His voice is like a rushing flood,
His word, a double blade,
Dividing soul from spirit clean,
And tearing strongholds made.

A crown upon His many crowns,
He rides the skies with might,
The Faithful One, the King of Kings,
The Judge, the Truth, the Light.

The sword comes forth, not forged by man,
But fire-breathed and true,
Each word He speaks breaks chains of sin,
And makes the dead brand new.

O tremble earth, before His eyes,
That burn with holy flame.
And rise, O saints, and lift your voice,

For Jesus is His name.

The King Is Coming!

His Eyes Are Like Fire.
His eyes are not soft with compromise. They are fire. They burn through pretense, through comfort, through the lies we cling to. They do not passively see, they consume, they refine, they purify.

His words do not flatter the flesh. They cut through it like a sword. They call out sin. They awaken hearts. They demand obedience.

He does not come riding a donkey this time. No humble gestures. No half measures. He comes riding a white horse, crowned with many crowns, with authority that shakes the heavens.

This is not the Jesus of culture. This is the Jesus of Revelation.
The triumphant King. The conquering Lion. The Judge who makes all things right.

Revelation 1:14-16 NIV - "The hair on His head was white like wool, as white as snow, and His eyes were like blazing fire. His feet were like bronze glowing in a furnace, and His voice was like the sound of rushing waters. In His right hand He held seven stars, and coming out of His mouth was a sharp, double-edged sword. His face was like the sun shining in all its brilliance."

This is the hour of fire. The hour of power. The hour of revival. Revival always begins with fire.

The fire in His eyes is not symbolic; it is the very essence of who He is. *Our God is a consuming fire (Hebrews 12:29).* This fire does not come to entertain or make us comfortable. It comes to burn what is unclean, to purify what religion could not, and to ignite a passion in your soul that cannot be contained.

You were not made to be lukewarm. Lukewarm hearts cannot withstand the fire. Lukewarm churches will not see revival. Lukewarm faith will not carry the glory of God.

This is not a time for half-hearted praise or shallow devotion. This is a time for hearts that burn, for trembling before God, for radical surrender that shakes the heavens. The fire comes to refine, not to destroy without purpose. It will burn pride, fear, and comfort. It will purify your motives, your desires, your very identity. The fire of God does not accept compromise, it produces pure, holy, relentless passion.

Hebrews 4:12 NIV - The Word of God is alive. It is active. It is sharper than any double-edged sword, cutting through soul and spirit, discerning the thoughts and intentions of the heart.

The Sword in His Mouth.
He does not carry the sword in His hand; He is the sword.

When He speaks, darkness flees. When He breathes, dead things rise. When He returns, nations will tremble before Him.

We are His hands, His feet, His voice until that day. Every word we speak in His name carries the weight of Heaven. When we preach His Word, we do not speak to tickle ears, we speak to break chains, to tear down strongholds, to release Heaven into earth.

The sword does not negotiate. It does not compromise. It exposes, it pierces, it conquers. And when His return comes, every tongue will confess, every knee will bow, every heart will be made known.

Until that moment, He has chosen you - your words, your obedience, your fire. Will you carry the sword boldly, or will it gather dust in your hands?

This Is the Hour of the Harvest. The fields are ready, but the laborers are few *(Matthew 9:37-38).* The world is burning with sin, and the harvest waits. This fire in your heart is not merely for comfort. It is to send you. It is to equip you. It is to ignite revival in every street, every neighborhood, and every life desperate for Jesus.

We were not saved to sit. We were saved to go, to carry the fire into the darkness, and to be living, breathing vessels of God's power.

You are called to be a burning lamp in this generation, not a dim light, not a flicker of hope, but a blazing beacon that cannot be ignored. You are called to lay hands on the sick, preach the gospel with boldness, release the power of God through demonstrations of the Spirit, and confront darkness wherever it dwells.

Holy Fire confronts sin. It destroys pride. It purifies hearts. It is not optional; it is essential for this hour.

Jesus Is Coming Back.
He is not returning to negotiate or make peace with compromise. He is coming back to take over. He is not looking for talent. He is looking for oil. *"Are your lamps burning?"* This is the question of eternity.

Have you been in the secret place, cultivating intimacy with Him, or have you been playing church? He is not looking for polished speeches, articulated performance, or good moral behavior. He is looking for warriors with hearts on fire, eyes on eternity, and hands in the harvest.

The time is now. The King is coming! The fire is coming!

Do not wait for revival to be handed to you. Do not wait for comfort to pass. Do not wait for the world to slow down. Step into the fire. Let your heart burn like His eyes. Let your words pierce like His sword. Let your life declare: *"The King is Coming!"*

Rise Up, Ignite The Flame!
Stop flirting with comfort. Stop entertaining compromise. Return to your first love. Let your life be on fire with the Spirit. Let your heart burn with conviction. Let your soul be consumed by the glory of God. This is your hour. This is your generation. This is your call.

RISE UP. BURN BRIGHT. BRING IN THE HARVEST.
For the eyes like fire are watching. And the sword is ready to speak.

www.ingramcontent.com/pod-product-compliance
Lightning Source LLC
Chambersburg PA
CBHW051542120626
46551CB00013B/1342